"GAELIC MADE EASY"

A Guide to Gaelic for Beginners

PART 1

COMPRISING 10 LESSONS IN GAELIC

Written and Compiled by

John M. Paterson

GAIRM PUBLICATIONS
29 Waterloo Street,
Glasgow G2 6BZ, Scotland

FOREWARD

This is the first part of a series of lessons published by the Gaelic League of Scotland for the benefit of their students and others who are studying the Gaelic. The lessons appeared originally in AN CEUM, a monthly now discontinued, and have been re-edited and where necessary amplified. The method of instruction employed was initiated by the League and has been found to be successful over a period of years. The remainder of the course has now been issued.

First Edition...........................1952
Third Edition (Revised).............1954
Fourth Edition........................1992
This impression......................1998

GAELIC MADE EASY PART 1

ISBN: 0-57970-548-0 text only
       0-88432-443-5 text and cassettes
       1-57970-124-8 text and cds

This edition published by Audio Forum
One Orchard Park Road, Madison, CT 06443 U.S.A.
www.audioforum.com

Printed in the United States of America

SOUND TABLE

A as in CAT. Never as in MATE.

E as in THEY or MET. Never as in ME.

I as in MACHINE or FIT. Never as in FIRE.

O as in GO or GOT.

U as in PUT or BUT. Never as in FUEL.

AO like EH-OO said quickly or NEUVE in French.

PH as F. Compare PHOTO in English.

BH and MH as V in Vat.

CH as in LOCH.

DH and GH as in UGH! back in throat.

SH and TH as H in HAT.

FH is silent except in three words FHEIN (hayn), FHUAIR (hoo-ir) and FHATHAST (ha-ast) where it has the sound of H.

IS as IS in MISSION i.e. ISH ; but IS meaning "is" is sounded ISS as in HISS.

SI as SI in MISSION i.e. SHI.

IDH and IGH as EE.

DHI and GHI as YE.

ANN sounds both "Ns" though often sounded as if A-OON.

L before A, O, U like LL in CALLING or THL.

MH and BH often sounded like W in middle of word, though, like V would also be correct.

I and E, when the second letters of a word, often sound like Y, as DIURA (dyura) i.e. almost a "j" sound ; but when an action-word is in past time this does not take place. LION! (lyeeon) Fill! but LION (leeon) Filled.

    Note: We use the "j" sound in the imitated pronunciation.

C in or at the end of a word is often sounded as CHK thus MAC as if it were MACHK, the CH sounded as in LoCH.

RT is often sounded as RST.

D and T. Get tongue well against back of upper front teeth. T is almost TH.

B and P and F. With lips well pressed together.

G well back in throat. GOT would be like UGOT.

IMITATED PRONUNCIATION

Sound CH as in loCH, ch as in church. O as in ʒO,
o as in got, ich as in which ; j as in jilt ; ing as in
sing ; ay as in day ; oo as in moon.

Only approximate pronunciation has been aimed at.
Anything more complex or detailed would only
confuse the learner.

LESSON 1

Gaelic is the national language of Scotland. It isn't hard to learn. The spelling looks a bit strange at first but don't worry, you'll pick it up all right. Thousands have mastered Gaelic. Add one more to the number and bring along others. Make Scotland once more a Gaelic Nation.

Take the word CAT. This means Cat or A Cat. You see there is no word for A in Gaelic. The Cat would be AN CAT, AN standing for The. MOR (pronounced like More in English or in some parts as Mor in Moral) means Big. Thus DORUS MOR, a big door, not Mor Dorus. Why? Because Gaelic always puts the person or thing spoken of first, and the word which describes, after.

Example—BORD TROM (**bord trOm**) a heavy table, LOCH FADA, a long loch. DUINE BEAG (**doon-ya-bek**), a little man. AN LA FUAR (**foo-ar**) the cold day. LA, Day and FUAR, Cold.

In Gaelic, as usually in English, the accent falls on the first syllable of the word. Custom is pronounced CUS-tom not cusTOM. Thus DORUS (**dorus**), a door is pronounced DOR-us not dorUS.

You will remember at school getting I am, Thou art, He, She or It is, We are, etc. Very well, Am, Art, etc. are all represented by the one little word THA (pr. **ha**) in Gaelic. Simple isn't it? But note this carefully. We write THA AN CAT MOR, The cat is big, not An cat tha mor as you would expect from the English. You see the important word in Gaelic is the one that tells the action or state, and next comes the person or thing concerned. Only in a case such as CO THA AIG AN DORUS? Who is at the door? does the rule appear to be broken.

Thus, He is cold, becomes, Is he cold. The boat will arrive, becomes, Will arrive the boat. John broke the window, Broke John the window. How then do you ask the question, Is the day cold? You will learn this in the next lesson, so be patient till then.

Examples—THA AN DORUS TROM, The door is heavy. THA AN LA FUAR, The day is cold. THA DUINE MOR AIG AN DORUS, A big man is, or There is a big man at the door. AIG (**ek**) at.

Learn—**MI** (**mee**) I. E (**eh**), He or It. I (**ee**), She or it. SINN (**sheeng**), We. SIBH (**sheev**), You. IAD (**ee-ut,** say quickly), They. It is pleasant to know that these words also mean Me, Him or It, Her or it, Us, You, Them, respectively. So much less to learn.

Examples—THA MI FUAR, I am cold. THA IAD SGITH (**skee**), They are tired.

BHA (**va**), stands for was, were, wert, or there was or were.

When in Gaelic you want to say a person "Has" anything you say, it is At him or her. Thus THA CU AIG IAIN, John has a dog. CU (**koo**), Dog.

In English they used to say long ago " I am a going, a coming," etc., and so it is in Gaelic.

THA MI A' DOL, I am a going. THA MI A' TIGHINN, I am a coming. A' is a short form for AIG meaning At. TIGHINN (**chee-ing**). DOL (**dol**) going.

Learn the following words and try your hand at the exercise which follows. In the imitated pronunciation **CH** is like CH in LOCH, and **ch** like ch in church, also **O** as in GO and **o** as in Got.

ACH (**aCH**), but. AGUS, and.

GANN (**ga-oon**), scarce.

TEINE (**chay-na**), a fire.

ARM, army.

BHA (**va**), was or were.

MO NIGHEAN (**mO nee-yan**), my daughter.

NIGHEAN also means girl.

EACH (**eCH**), horse.

SEUMAS (**Shay-mus**), James

IAIN (**ee-yayn**). John.
MAIRI (**ma-ee-ree**), Mary.
DACHAIDH (**daCH-y**), home, also written DHACH-
  AIDH (**GHaCH-y**).
TE (**tay**), tea.
SIUCAR (**shooCH-kar**), sugar.
BAINNE (**ban-ya**), milk.
GUAL (**gooal**), coal.
TAIGH (**ta-ee**), house.
LAMH (**lav**), hand.
LAMHAN (**lav-an**), hands.
GLAN, Clean.
AN NOCHD, (**noCHk**) to-night (note CHD sounds
  CHK).
Mo (**mO**), my ; UR (**oor**), your.
DEAS (**jayss**), ready.
GASDA, fine.
DO (do as in **dot**), to.
SGOIL (**skol**), school.
MAR SIN (**mar shin**), so.
ANNS (**a-oons**), in, is used before AN meaning The.
A NIS (**nish**), now.
AS (**ass**), out.
GILLE (**geel-ya**, G as in get, boy.
BLATH (**bla**), say quickly, warm.
FLIUCH (**flooCH**), wet.
SALACH (**sal-aCH**), dirty.
SGITH (**skee**), tired.
CUIR (**kooir**), put.
AIR (**err**), on.
CO? (**kO**), Who?
-SA; added for emphasis.

Gaelic to English

Tha mi fuar. Tha i sgith. Tha iad fuar agus fliuch.
Tha an la blath. Tha sinn deas a nis. Tha an loch
fada. Co bha aig an dorus? Bha duine mor. Co bha
air an each? Bha Iain beag. Bha cu mor agus cat
beag aig Seumas. Tha an gille beag a' tighinn. Bha
an la fuar agus mar sin bha an cu agus an cat aig an

teine. Tha ur te deas a nis. Gasda, tha mi a' tighinn.
Tha mo nighean a' tighinn dachaidh an nochd. Bha i
anns an arm. Cuir siucar agus bainne anns an te.
Cuir gual air an teine, tha e a' dol as. Tha an gual
gann a nis. Bha ur lamhan glan ach bha mo lamhan-
sa salach. Tha e blath a nis. Bha an gille beag a'
dol do an sgoil. Bha taigh mor aig Mairi. Bha cu
beag aig mo nighean.

Translation

I am cold. She is tired. They are cold and wet.
The day is warm. We are ready now. The loch is long.
Who was at the door? A big man was, i.e. It was a
big man. Who was on the horse? Little John was,
i.e. It was little John. James had a big dog and a
little cat. The little boy is coming. The day was cold
and so the dog and the cat were at the fire. Your tea
is ready now. Fine, I am coming. My daughter is
coming home to-night. She was in the army. Put
sugar and milk in the tea. Put coal on the fire, it is
going out. The coal is scarce now. Your hands were
clean but my hands were dirty. It is warm now. The
little boy was going to the school. Mary had a big
house. My daughter had a little dog.

LESSON 2

We saw in the last lesson that John is cold, is written in Gaelic THA IAIN FUAR, the Is being put at the beginning. Suppose now we want to ask the question, Is John cold? we will put BHEIL (**vayl**) in place of THA. Thus we get, BHEIL IAIN FUAR? In the same way, Are you going home? would be BHEIL SIBH A' DOL DACHAIDH. When reading a Gaelic book, however, you will notice that the word AM is usually placed before BHEIL. This is merely to stress the fact that a question is being asked. So you would see our sentences written as AM BHEIL IAIN FUAR? AM BHEIL SIBH A' DOL DACHAIDH? It is better for the learner to use the AM form.

BHEIL has the same meanings as THA, i.e. Am, art, is, are.

Notice this common saying C'AIT' AM BHEIL SIBH A'DOL? meaning, Where are you going? C'AIT'? (**kach**), where?

Now we are getting a move on towards conversation. We shall try to put into Gaelic such expressions as:

I am sorry that you are going home.

I am sorry that you are not coming.

DUILICH (**dool-eeCH**), sorry; a very useful word this. GUM (**goom**), stands for That; and NACH (**naCH**) for the two words That not; and by the way both GUM and NACH take BHEIL instead of THA after them. Thus we have THA MI DUILICH GUM BHEIL SIBH A' DOL DACHAIDH, I am sorry that you are going home. THA MI DUILICH NACH 'EIL SIBH A' TIGHINN. I am sorry that you are not coming.

Do **not** write GUM THA SIBH, etc. Note also that we have written NACH 'EIL. The BH (V sound) has

7

been dropped and an apostrophe put in, for NACH BHEIL is rather an un-musical sound. Dropping a V sound occurs also in English as **O'er** for Over. 'EIL (**ayl**).

Here is another common word, THEAGAMH (**hek-av**) ; meaning It may be, or Perhaps. It is followed by GUM or NACH.

THEAGAMH GUM BHEIL AN GILLE FUAR, It may be that the boy is cold. THEAGAMH NACH 'EIL AN COTA DEAS, It may be that the coat is not ready (or finished). COTA, Coat (**kota**).

Finally, how do we say in Gaelic a phrase like It is not cold to-night. The answer is CHAN 'EIL E FUAR AN NOCHD. The 'EIL is of course BHEIL coming after CHA, meaning Not. CHA takes an N, i.e. CHAN before A, E, I, O, U, just as we say in English, An apple, eye, etc. CHA (**CHa**), CHAN, not. It always comes first in your sentence. CHAN 'EIL (**CHan yayl**).

Examples — CHAN 'EIL UR LAMHAN GLAN, Your hands are not clean. CHAN 'EIL UISGE ANNS AN TAIGH, There isn't (there's no) water in the house. UISGE (**oosh-ka**), water.

Is there a word for Yes or for No in Gaelic? There is not, but read the following very carefully.

AM BHEIL BAINNE ANNS AN TE? Is there milk in the tea?

CHAN 'EIL (BAINNE ANNS AN TE), There is not (milk in the tea).

THA (BAINNE ANNS AN TE). There is (milk in the tea).

What has happened? Well, we have answered the question in almost the same words in which it was asked. So now you will see that there is no single word in Gaelic for Yes or No. You must repeat the saying or doing word, but just as in English, so in Gaelic, you leave out in your answer any words that are not needed. In the above case these would be, BAINNE ANNS AN TE, i.e. Milk in the tea.

8

AM BHEIL SIBH A' DOL DO EIRE AN NOCHD?
Are you going to Eire to-night? Answer, THA, I am,
CHAN 'EIL, I am not. You will notice that even MI,
as well as A' DOL DO EIRE AN NOCHD is left out.

Learn the following words

IDIR (**ee-jir**), at all.
MILIS (**meel-ish**), sweet.
GED (**get**), although.
TETH (**chay**), hot.
GU LEOIR (**goo lyor**), plenty, enough.
GU TRIC (**goo treeCHk**), often, accent on TRIC.
CLUICH (**kloo-eeCH**), playing.
RATHAD (**ra-ad**), road.
EAGLAIS (**ekl-ish**), church.
CAR, a bit, somewhat.
AN DIUGH (**an-joo**), to-day, stress on DIUGH.
FHATHAST (**ha-ast**), yet.
SIABUNN (**shee-a-bun**), soap.
AM MAIREACH (**am-mar-aCH**), to-morrow. Accent
    on MAIR.
C'AR SON (**kar son**), why? Accent on SON.
BIDH (**be-ee**), shall or will be.
BATA MOR, a big boat (**baa-ta mOr**), accent on MOR.
FAGAIL (**fag-il**), leaving.
CINNTEACH (**keen-chaCH**), sure.
A or AS (**ass**), from, or out of.
ALBA (**al-up-a**), Scotland. Accent on AL.
SASUNN (**Sas-unn**), England.
GAIDHLIG (**gaa-leek**), Gaelic.
NOLLAIG (**nol-lig**), Christmas.
AN DE (**an jay**), yesterday, stress on DE.

Gaelic to English

   Am bheil sibh sgith? Chan ˙ il idir (omit mi).
Tha e fuar an diugh ach bha e ˡ ᵤth gu leoir an de.
Bidh e fluich am maireach. Ged tha e blath, tha
uisge gu leoir anns an loch fhathast. Cuir uisge teth
anns an te, Iain: tha e car fuar. Am bheil e milis gu

9

leoir? Tha e gasda. Bidh bata mor a' fagail Alba am maireach. Tha an duine salach. Theagamh gum bheil siabunn agus uisge gann. Am bheil Gaidhlig aig Seumas? Tha, ach tha mi cinnteach nach 'eil Gaidhlig aig Mairi. C'ar son? Tha i a Sasunn. C'ait' am bheil Iain a' dol? Tha e a' dol do'n (do an) sgoil ach tha e gu tric a' cluich air an rathad. Am bheil sibh a' tighinn do'n eaglais an diugh? Tha mi duilich nach 'eil. Tha e car fuar agus tha mi sgith. Bidh mo nighean a'dol dachaidh aig Nollaig.

Translation

Are you tired? Not at all i.e. I am not at all. It is cold to-day but it was warm enough yesterday. It will be wet to-morrow. Though it is warm, there is plenty water in the loch yet. Put hot water in the tea, Iain: it is somewhat cold. Is it sweet enough? It is fine. A big boat will be leaving Scotland to-morrow. The man is dirty. Perhaps soap and water are scarce. Has James Gaelic? i.e. Is Gaelic at James? There is but I am certain that Mary has not i.e. there is not Gaelic at Mary. Why? She is from England. Where is John going? He is going to the school but he is often playing on the road. Are you coming to the church to-day? I am sorry that I am not. It is a bit cold and I am tired. My daughter will be going home at Christmas.

LESSON 3

Most people have heard of Dumbarton, one of the oldest towns in Scotland. The name is Gaelic and means The Fort of the Britons. It should really be spelt Dunbarton for DUN (**doon**) meaning A Fort is the first part of the name. It would appear that people found it easier to say DUM than DUN before the letter B of Barton. This happens throughout Gaelic. Thus we say AM BORD, The Table, for AN BORD and AM (not AN) BATA, The Boat. Three other letters M, P, F, change an N to an M. So we find AM (for AN) MAIREACH, The (or To-) Morrow, AM (for AN) PARTAN, The Crab and AM (for AN) FEASGAR (**fesk-ar**), The evening, also AM (for AN) BHEIL.

The reader will also understand why we write GUM (for the usual GUN) BHEIL E A' TIGHINN and will not be surprised to see GUN and AN changing to GUM and AM before the letters B, F, M, P

One o her small point worth a passing notice. THA MI A' TIGHINN means I am (a) coming, the A' being short for AIG, at. With a word like OL, (**ol**) drinking, we write AG instead of A' for the sake of the sound.

Examples—THA MAIRI AG OL BAINNE, Mary is drinking milk. This G is put in before our old friends of the schoolroom A, E, I, O, U, and curiously enough before RADH (**ra**) meaning Saying.

THA DOMHNALL AG IARRAIDH SGAILEAN-UISGE, Donald is looking for an umbrella.

THA ANNA AG RADH NACH 'EIL SGAILEAN-UISGE ANNS AN TAIGH, Anna says that there is not an umbrella in the house. DOMHNALL (**Do-nal**) Donald. IARRAIDH (**eear-ee**), seeking, looking for, enquiring. SGAILEAN-UISGE (**sgalan-oosh-ka**) umbrella.

We saw how THA was replaced by BHEIL (or 'EIL) after AM, CHA, GUM and NACH. Now you may ask, does BHA change also after these words? It does, it becomes ROBH (**rO**, the bh being silent).

Examples—BHA AN ᴅUINE FUAR. The man was cold, (AN) ROBH AN DUINE FUAR? Was the man cold?

BHA AN DORSAIR AG RADH GUN ROBH E FUAR. The door-keeper was saying that he was cold. DORSAIR (**dor-sir**).

Note—GUN (not GUM) ROBH also AN (not AM) ROBH. AN ROBH AN AIMSIR BRIAGH AN DIURA AN DE? Was the weather fine in Jura yesterday?

Answer—BHA, It was, or CHA ROBH, It was not. The full answer would be BHA (or CHA ROBH) AN AIMSIR BRIAGH, but just as in English, we drop unnecessary words in our reply.

AIMSIR (**em-shir**), weather. DIURA (**joo-ra**), Jura. BRIAGH (**bree-a**: gh silent), fine.
AN DE (**jay**), yesterday.

Note—We change AN meaning In, to ANNS before The in Gaelic. Thus we say ANNS AN TAIGH not AN AN TAIGH; ANNS AN ABHAINN In the river; but AN DIURA in Jura.
ABHAINN (**av-ing**), river.

Three very common words are SEO (**sho**), This or These. SIN (**shin**), That or Those. SUD or SIUD (both pr. **shoot**), or UD (**oot**) all three meaning Yon or Yonder.

Note their curious use—

Examples—AN GILLE, The boy: AN GILLE SEO, This boy. AN GILLE SIN, That boy. AN GILLE UD yon(der) boy. UD is preferred here to SUD.

Now when AN meaning The, refers to more than one person or thing we change it to NA. AN GILLE,

The boy would become NA GILLEAN, The boys.
So we have NA GILLEAN SEO, These boys. NA
GILLEAN SIN, Those boys and NA GILLEAN UD,
Yon(der) boys. GILLEAN (**geel-yan**), boys.

Learn the following words

LOCH (**loCH**), Loch. LOCHAN, lochs.
IASG (**ee-asg**), a fish.
NIALL (**Nyee-al**), Neil.
IASGACH (**eeasg-aCH**), fishing.
INBHIR NIS (**inver-nish**), Inverness.
DUIN (**dooin**), close. NA DUIN, don't close.
FOSGAIL (**foskil**), open. NA FOSGAIL, don't open.
This NA is different from the NA meaning 'The,'
   though spelt the same.
UINNEAG (**oon-yag**), window.
TAPADH LEAT (**tapa let**), thank you.
TAPADH LEIBH (**layv**), thank you (said to one,
   senior in age or rank).
FHUAIR (**hoo-ir**), found or got.
SPARAN, a purse.
AN UAIR A (**oo-ir**), when or the time that.
CHAIDH (**CHa-ee**), went.
THUIRT (**hoo-irt**), said.
SILEADH (**sheel-uGH**), raining, the "ugh" is deep in
   throat.
UILLEAM (**ooil-yam**), William.
TOG (**tOg**), lift.
A H-UILE (**a hool-a**), every.
TOILICHTE (**tol-eeCH-chay**), pleased.
OBAIR (**Ob-ir**), working.
A RITHIST (**ree-isht**), again.
CATRIONA (**kat-reena**). Accent on -reena.

Gaelic to English

Am bord seo. An cu sin. An duine ud. Na lamhan
sin. An loch fada seo. Na lochan fada ud. An robh
sibh ag iasgach an diugh? Cha robh, bha an la fuar.
Cha robh Domhnall aig an taigh an de. C'ait' an

robh e? Bha Niall ag radh gun robh e an Inbhir Nis.
Duin an dorus Anna, agus fosgail an uinneag. Tapadh
leat. Fhuair an gille beag seo sparan air an rathad an
uair a bha e a' dol do'n sgoil. Chaidh an teine as.
Thuirt Mairi nach robh gual anns an taigh. An uair a
bha iad an Sasunn an robh an aimsir briagh? Cha
robh idir. Bha e a' sileadh a h-uile la. Bha Catriona
toilichte gun robh Uilleam ag obair a rithist. Na cuir
gual air an teine, Iain. Na tog an sparan sin.

Translation

This table. That dog. Yon man. Those hands.
This long loch. Yon loch lochs. Were you fishing
to-day? I was not, the day was cold. Donald was
not at the house (also "at home") yesterday. Where
was he? Neil was saying that he was in Inverness.
Shut the door Anna, and open the window. Thank
you. This little boy found a purse on the road when
he was going to the school. The fire went out. Mary
said that there wasn't coal in the house. When they
were in England was the weather fine? It was not at
all. It was raining every day. Catriona was pleased
that William was working again. Don't put coal on
the fire, Iain (i.e. John). Don't lift that purse.

LESSON 4

A gentleman went into a tailor's shop to enquire about a coat he had left the week before to have a small repair made. He said to the tailor AM BI AN COTA DEAS AN DIUGH? Will the coat be ready to-day? and the tailor replied, THA MI DUILICH NACH BI AN COTA DEAS AN DIUGH ACH BIDH E DEAS AM MAIREACH. I am sorry that the coat will not be ready to-day but it will be ready to-morrow.

Now the first thing that will strike you is that we have used two somewhat different words for "will be" namely BIDH (**be-ee**) a long form, and BI (**be**) a short form. The short form is used after our old acquaintances, AM, GUM and NACH.

Examples — AM BI IAIN A' TIGHINN DACH-AIDH AN NOCHD? Will Iain be coming home to-night?

THA E COLTACH GUM BI (omit the rest). It is likely that he will be. COLTACH (**kol-taCH**) likely.

Of course the answer might have been simply,. He will be, or He will not be. · These replies could be as follows: BIDH or CHA BHI (E A' TIGHINN DACHAIDH AN NOCHD) being understood.

The thing that will puzzle you here is CHA BHI. You expected CHA BI. The reason is that when CHA comes before any word beginning with a B it changes the B sound to that of a V and this is spelt in Gaelic BH. BHI sounds like Ve in Veto. Later on you will find that a few other letters have their sound changed when CHA comes before them. It works out very easily however. Just note, though, that CHA does not take the long form BIDH after it.

Let us go back to the question the gentleman put to the tailor. AM BI AN COTA DEAS AN DIUGH?

Will the coat be ready to-day? He could also have put the question this way, " Will the coat not be ready to-day? " Now you see he's asking a question and at the same time he feels that the tailor will reply that it will not be ready. What we want now is a word that will stand for AM (or AN) the question word, and CHA which means Not. The word we are seeking for is NACH (**naCH**), the same word which we already saw stood for " That not " in the middle of a sentence. And further it takes the short form BI after it when it means Shall be or Will be.

The question in its second form will run thus:— NACH BI AN COTA DEAS AN DIUGH? Will the coat not be ready to-day? or Will not the coat be ready to-day?

Examples — NACH BI E FLIUCH AM MAIR-EACH AN GRIANAIG? Will it not be wet to-morrow in Greenock? BIDH, It will be. CHA BHI, It will not be THEAGAMH GUM BI, Perhaps (that) it will be. THEAGAMH NACH BI, Perhaps (that) it will not be, (E FLIUCH, etc.) being understood in replies. NACH ROBH AN RIGH AN GLASCHU AN DE? Was not the king in Glasgow yesterday?

Answer—BHA, He was. CHA ROBH, He was not RIGH (**ree**) King.

Learn these words

GRIANAIG (**greean-ek**). Greenock.
TUIGSINN (**toog-sheeng**), understanding. NA, what: also " The." See Lesson 3.
DONA (**dona**) bad, MATH (**ma**) good.
TAILLEAR (**tàl-yar**), tailor.
AIR SON (**er son**), for.
DI-SATHUIRN (**jee-sa-hoorn**), Saturday. Accent on SA.
CHUNNAIC (**CHoon-ek**), saw.
SRAID (**sraj**), street.
SRUIGHLEA (**sroola**), Stirling.
CREIDSINN (**kret-sheeng**), believing, thinking.

16

TAIGH DHEALBH (**Ta-ee Ya-luv**), picture-house.
SEOMAR (**sho-mar**), room.
FAOTAINN (**foo-ting**), getting.
MAIGHSTIR (**maee-styrr**), master.
DACHAIDH often written DHACHAIDH (**GHaCHy**),
  home, homewards.
FALBH (**fal-uv**), go away, or going away.
AIR FALBH, away or off.
MORAG (**mO-rag**), Sarah.
AIR AIS (**er-ash**), back. Stress is on AIS.
AN DRASDA, at present, now.
TILLEADH (**cheel-yuGH**), returning.
ROIMH (**ro-ee**), before.
FAICINN (**feCH-king**), seeing.
FRASACH (**fras-aCH**), showery.
GU TROM (**goo trOm**), heavily. Note GU = "ly".
  Accent on TROM.
AN RAOIR (**an ra-wir**), last night.
AN UIRIDH (**oor-ee**), last year.
TINN (**cheeng**), sick.
TIR (**cheer**), land, country.

Gaelic to English

    Chan 'eil mi a' tuigsinn na tha e ag radh. Nach bi
an cota deas air son Di-Sathuirn? Tha e coltach nach
bi. C' ait' an robh sibh a' dol an uair a chunnaic mi
sibh an Sraid Iain? Tha mi a' creidsinn gun robh mi
a' dol do'n taigh-dhealbh. Nach 'eil an seomar seo
fuar? Tha am maighstir ag radh gum bheil an gual
a tha e a' faotainn an drasda dona agus gum bheil an
gual math a' dol as an tir. Nach bi Morag a' dol
do'n sgoil an diugh? Cha bhi, tha i tinn. Am bi e
a' tilleadh dhachaidh a rithist? Cha bhi e a' tilleadh
roimh Nollaig. Tha mi a' faicinn gum bi an la
frasach. Bha e a' sileadh gu trom an raoir. Chunnaic
mi am bata a' falbh an raoir. Tha na gillean air
falbh do Inbhir Nis an diugh. Am bi Anna agus
Mairi a' tighinn an nochd? Cha bhi. Bha Domhnall
ag radh nach bi iad a' tighinn an rathad seo idir.

Translation

I am not understanding i.e. I don't understand what he is saying. Will the coat not be ready for Saturday? It is likely that it will not be. Where were you going when I saw you in John Street? I believe I was going to the picture-house. (Note: "that" in Gaelic must not be left out). Is this room not cold? The master is saying that the coal that he is getting at present is bad and that the good coal is going out the country. Will Morag not be going to the school to-day? She will not, she is sick. Will he be returning home again? He will not be returning before Christmas. I see that the day will be showery. It was raining heavily last night. I saw the boat going away last night. The boys are off to Inverness to-day. Will Anna and Mary be coming to-night? They will not. Donald was saying that they will not be coming this way (or road) at all.

LESSON 5

AN SGRIOBH SIBH AN LITIR SIN AN NOCHD? said the Master to the Clerk. Perhaps you will have guessed that the Master meant "Will you write that letter to-night?" but would like to know how the phrase was put together. Here is the way and it will serve for all such phrases. Start from SGRIOBH! (**skreev**), Write! the word which gives the order. It may be used, however, in a milder way, thus AN SGRIOBH SIBH AN LITIR SIN AN NOCHD? Will you write that letter to-night? which is simply asking a civil question. Or we might say NACH SGRIOBH SIBH AN LITIR SIN AN NOCHD? Will you not write that letter to-night? LITIR (**lee-chir**) letter.

The Clerk, in a hurry home, AIG COIG UAIREAN (5 o'clock) may say CHA SGRIOBH (MI, etc., being omitted) I shall not. But if he intends to write it, he will say SGRIOBHAIDH (**skreev-ee**). In a reply the rest of the phrase of course is understood. What we have done is to add AIDH (**ee**) to the short form, SGRIOBH which was really the word of order. But when do we use the short form? The answer is, after AN (or AM), NACH, CHA and also our old friends GUN (GUM) and NACH.

TOG AM MAL! Lift the rent! TOGAIDH AN CLEIREACH (**klay-raCH**) AM MAL. The clerk will lift the rent.

CHA TOG AN CLEIREACH AM MAL. The clerk will not lift the rent. MAL (**maal**), rent.

THA AM MAOR-TAIGHE AG RADH GUN TOG AN CLEIREACH AM MAL. The house factor says that the clerk will lift the rent. MAOR-TAIGHE (**moor-ta-ee**) house-factor.

AN TOG AN CLEIREACH AM MAL? Will the clerk lift the rent?

CHA TOG, He will not. TOGAIDH, He will. These two are in answer to the preceding question.

Note that in words like BRIS! (**breesh**) Break! CUIR! Put! DEASAICH! (**jay-seeCH**), Prepare! (or Bake!) where the last vowel is an "I" we add nly IDH to the order word. Thus: BRISIDH E AN UINNEAG, He will break the window. CUIRIDH MI GEALL (**gyall**) AIR SIN; I shall put a bet on that. DEASAICHIDH I BONNACH; She will bake a cake. SIN (**Shin**) That DEASAICHIDH (**jay-seeCH-ee**).

Always stress the first syllable of Gaelic words.

CHA is a word which may give you a little trouble if you are not careful for it sometimes changes the sound of the word that comes after it. In last lesson we saw how when CHA came before BI it made the B sound into a V sound which was shown by writing BH for B. Now the letters that CHA changes in this way are B, F, M, P, and C, G, S. They are written with an H after them. Remember that BH and MH sound like **V**. PH as in **photo**: FH is silent: CH as in lo**CH**: SH and TH like **H** in hat: GH as in **UGH**, guttural, back in your throat.

Examples—BUAIL! (**boo-il**) strike! CHA BHUAIL SINN AN CU. We shall not strike the dog. CUIR! (**kooir**), put! CHA CHUIR MI EARBSA (**er-ub-sa**) AN IAIN. I will not put confidence in Iain. GABH! (**gav**) take! CHA GHABH IAD TE NO CAFE. They will not take tea or coffee. FAN! stay. CHAN FHAN AN CU SAMHACH (**sav-aCH**). The dog will not stay quiet. FH is silent so that FHAN sounds simply **AN**. We write CHAN just as you would say **an apple** and not a apple.

Learn these words

DI-LUAIN (**jee-loo-ayn**), Monday. Accent on LU.
BOIRIONNACH (**bor-un-nach**), woman.
CROSDA, bad tempered.
CEANNAICH (**kyan-eeCH**), buy. AONTA (**oon-ta**), lease.

AIR, on it. ANN, in it.
SEOLTA (**sholt-ta**), wide-awake, cute.
TEARLACH (**cher-laCH**), Charles.
BOIDHEACH (**boy-aCH**), bonnie.
TILL (**cheel**), return.
GU BRATH (**braaCH**), ever, or for ever.
DIRICH (**jee-reeCH**), climb.
BEINN (**baynn**), Ben, peak.
LAOMUINN (**loo-ming**), Lomond.
A CHIONN (**CHyun**), because.
CEO (**kyo**), mist.
SGIAN (**skee-an**), knife.
UMHAIL (**oo-ul**), obedient.
A ATHAIR (**a-hir**), his father.
SUIM (**soo-im**), heed.
MAC (**maCHK**), son.
CAILEAG (**kalag**), CAILEAGAN, girl, girls.
AN SEO (**sho**), here.
EILIDH (**ayl-ee**), Helen. Use SIBH to your elders.
RO LEISG (**rO layshk**), too, rather lazy.
THU (**oo not hoo**), Thou, thee, familiar form.
LEIG! (**lyayk**), let!
AS (**ass**), out, away in sense of "off".
SUAS (**sooas**), up, upwards (motion).
SIOS (**sheeas**), down downwards (motion).
COPAN (**kO-pan**), cup.
FAR, In the place that, where.
GUS (**goose**), Until, followed by AN (AM) or NACH
  i.e. the two question words.
CEUM (**kaym**), step, walk.
AN EARAR (**un-yerrur**), The day after to-morrow.
ROP (**rop**), rope.
ALASDAIR (**al-as-dir**), Alexander.

Gaelic to English

Am bi ur mac a' tighinn dachaidh am maireach?
Cha bhi e an seo roimh an earar. Am bris Alasdair
an gual? Cha bhris, tha e ro leisg. Cha bhuail am
boirionnach an cu mor, crosda sin. Chan fhan an
gille anns an taigh. An ceannaich iad am buth? Cha

cheannaich ach gabhaidh iad aonta air. Tha iad
seolta. O nach till Tearlach Boidheach a rithist?
Cha till gu brath. An dirich na caileagan Beinn
Laomuinn an diugh? Cha dirich a chionn gum bheil
an la fliuch agus an ceo trom. C'ar son nach cuir
an gille beag sin an sgian sios? Chan 'eil e umhail
do a athair. Cha ghabh e suim do na tha e ag radh.
Fan an seo gus an till mi. Cuir as an solus. Leig
as an rop. An gabh thu copan te, Eilidh? Gabhaidh,
tapadh leat, ach na cuir siucar no bainne ann. Fan
far am bheil thu. Gabhaidh mi ceum suas an rathad.
Gus am bris an la.

Translation

Will your son be coming home to-morrow? He will
not be here before the day after. Will Alexander
break the coal? He will not, he is too lazy. The
woman will not hit that big, bad-tempered dog. The
boy will not stay in the house. Will they buy the
shop? They will not but they will take a lease on it.
They are wide-awake. O will Bonnie Charlie not
come back again? He will never return. Will the
girls climb Ben Lomond to-day? They will not
because (that) the day is wet and the mist heavy.
Why will that little boy not put the knife down? He
is not obedient to (he does not obey) his father.
He doesn't (won't) give heed to what he says. Stay
here till I come back. Put out the light. Let go the
rope. Will you take a cup of tea, Helen? I will,
thanks, but don't put sugar or milk in it. Stay where
you are. I'll take a walk up the road. Till the day
breaks.

LESSON 6

We have already come across little phrases like AIG AN DORUS, at the door ; AIR AN TEINE, on the fire ; ANNS AN ABHAINN, in the river. Likewise we have LEIS AN DUINE, by (or with) the man. By the way, LE meaning **by** or **with,** takes the long form LEIS when it comes before AN or AM or NA meaning "the". LEIS **(laysh)**. Thus LE DUINE, by (or with) a man, but LEIS AN DUINE, by (or with) the man. In the same way AN, in, becomes ANNS ; and RI, close to, becomes RIS. RI TOBAR, at a well ; RIS AN TOBAR, at the well. RIS **(reesh)**. RI **(ree)** ; LE **(lay)**.

Well, now, suppose the word that comes after AIG AN, AIR AN, etc., begins with a C or G or our old friends B, M, P, we put an H after the first letter of the word thus changing its sound slightly. Take for example CEANN **(kya-oon)** head. AIR AN CHEANN **(CHya-oon)**, on the head. AIR AM BHORD **(vord)** is in the same way, on the table. But in speaking it has become the custom to drop the N or M of AN or AM and so in speaking and writing we have AIR A' CHEANN, on the head. AIR A' BHORD, on the table. BHA E A' COISEACHD LEIS A' CHU ANNS A' PHAIRC, he was walking with the dog in the park. COISEACHD **(kosh-aCHk)**, walking ; PAIRC **(parCHk)**, park. But THA AN CRODH ANNS AN FHRAOCH, the cattle are in the heather. CRODH **(crO)**, cattle ; FRAOCH **(frooCH)**, heather. FHRAOCH **(rooCH)**, the FH being silent.

Notice what happens when we are dealing with a word like FEAR **(fer)**, man. When a vowel, A, E, I, O, U, comes after the F we write AIG AN, LEIS AN, etc., not AIG A', LEIS A', etc. THA TAIGH MOR AIG AN FHEAR **(eg an yer)**, the man has a big house.

You see, with FH silent the word really begins now with a vowel sound, and so we have AN and not A'.

This is just like CHA becoming CHAN before 'EIL and in English A apple becoming AN APPLE.

23

BIDH IAD AIG AN TAIGH-DHEALBH ANNS AN FHEASGAR, They will be at the picture-house in the evening. Feasgar (**fes-kar**), evening.

Also, N coming before e is sounded usually as NY : hence **n yer.** In referring to a number of persons both male and female we use DUINE. FEAR, only if all male.

Here are a few small but very useful words: DO (**do**), to ; Fo (**fo**), under , O (**o**) (or BHO sounded **vo**), from ; ROIMH (**ro-ee**), before ; TROIMH (**tro-ee**), through.

These all take AN (or 'N for short) after them.

THUG I COPAN TE DO 'N FHEAR, she gave a cup of tea to the man. SAIGHDEAR (**saee-jar**) soldier. SAIGHDEARAN, soldiers. CHAIDH NA SAIGHDEARAN TROIMH 'N FHASACH, the soldiers went through the desert. CHAIDH (**CHa-ee**), went. FASACH, desert. THUG (**hook**), gave, brought.

Name words that begin with S are worth noticing. Take, for instance, these three : SRAID (**sraj**), street ; SAOR (**soor**), joiner ; SEARRAG (**sharag**), bottle.

CHUNNAIC MI IAIN AIR AN T-SRAID, I saw John on the street. T-SRAID (**traj**). Although S is kept in when writing, it is not sounded.

Note insertion of -T before S.

THA LOCAIR AIG AN T-SAOR, the joiner has a plane ; LOCAIR (**loCH-kir**), plane ; AIG AN T-SAOR (**eg an toor**).

CUIR FION ANNS AN T-SEARRAG, put wine in the bottle ; T-SEARRAG (**char-ag**). FION (**fee-on**) wine.

But words beginning with SG, SP, SM, ST make no change.

SGAOIL MAIRI IM AIR AN ARAN LEIS AN SGIAN, Mary spread butter on the bread with the knife ; SGAOIL (**sgooil**), spread. MADUINN (**ma-ting**), morning. IM (**eem**), butter. ARAN, bread.

Learn these words

COILLE (**kyle-ya**), wood.
AN SIN, Then, after that, also means There (place).

24

RAINIG (**ran-eek**), reached, arrived. CAR, car.
A MACH (**maCH**), out (motion).
A STEACH (**styaCH**), in (motion).
PAIPEAR-NAIGHEACHD (**paee-par nay-aCHk**),
   newspaper.
BAILE (**bal-a**), town.
RI MIRE (**ree meer-a**), at play.
LOCHAN, pond.
SNEACHD (**shnyeCHk**), snow.
CRAOBH (**kroov**), tree. CRAOBHAN (**kroovan**),
   trees.
TIORAM (**chir-am**), dry.
AIR SON (**son**), for.

Gaelic to English

Fhuair e sparan air an t-sraid. Tha Mairi a' dol
do'n phairc leis a' chu. Bha e fuar agus fliuch anns a'
mhaduinn ach bha e tioram anns an fheasgar. Bha
na gillean a' cluich anns a' choille. Am bi sibh a' dol
a mach anns a' bhata an nochd? Cha bhi, tha an
aimsir dona. Thug am boirionnach am mal do'n
chleireach an diugh. Chunnaic mi anns a' phaipear-
naigheachd gun robh sneachd trom anns a' bhaile an
raoir. Bha an cu ri mire leis a' chat. Rainig an car
Inbhir Nis roimh an fheasgar. Am bheil thu a'
tighinn a steach a nis Anna? Chan 'eil. Tha mi
a' dol do'n tobar air son uisge agus an sin, cuiridh
mi a mach an crodh.

Translation

He found a purse on the street. Mary is going to
the park with the dog. It was cold and wet in the
morning but it was dry in the evening. The boys were
playing in the wood. Will you be going out in the
boat to-night? I won't, the weather is bad. The
woman gave the rent to the clerk to-day. I saw in the
newspaper that there was heavy snow in the town last
night. The dog was playing with the cat. The car
reached Inverness before the evening. Are you coming
in now, Anna? I am not (i.e. No). I am going to the
well for water and then I will put out the cattle.

LESSON 7

To say a thing happens in Past Time in Gaelic, take the Doing-word and put an H after the first letter.

Example—BRIS! Break! BHRIS E AN COPAN, He broke the cup. CUM! Hold! CHUM IAD AN ROP, They held the rope. CHUM (**CHoom**).

But if the word begins with a vowel you put DH' in front of it.

Example—OL! Drink! DH' OL SINN AM FION, We drank the wine. INNIS! (**een-ish**) Tell! DH'INNIS I SGEUL, She told a story.

DH'INNIS (**yeenish**). DH' OL (**GHol**). FION (**fee-on**). SGEUL (**skayl**), story.

Note that DH before E or I sounds like Y in English, and that before A, O, U, is like GH in uGH!

Words beginning with F may give a little trouble if you are not careful. Take these two:—FREAGAIR! (**frek-ir**), Answer! and FOSGAIL! Open! FHREA-GAIR E AN DUINE, He answered the man. (FH is silent so **rek-ir**). FHOSGAIL, however, with the FH silent has the vowel O as its first sound, so, as in the case of OL, we put DH' in front. Though the FH is not sounded it must be kept in when writing.

Example — DH' FHOSGAIL (**GHOsk-il**) MI AN DORUS, I opened the door. DH' FHAG E AN CAR AIG AN TAIGH-OSDA, He left the car at the inn. FAG! leave! DH' FHAG (**GHak**), left. CAR, Car. TAIGH-OSDA, inn.

In short, you will treat words commencing with F followed by a vowel just as we have done with FOSGAIL and FAG.

The easiest words to work with are those beginning with L, N, R, or an S followed by G, M, P or T. They don't change at all. LION! (**lyeen**), Fill! LION (**leen**), filled. NIGH (**nyee**), Wash! NIGH (**nee**), Washed. Note difference in sound, however, of NIGH and LION in past time. RUITH! (**roo-ee**), Run! RUITH, Ran. STAD! Stop! STAD! Stopped. SPION! (**speeon**), Pluck! SPION, Plucked. SMAOINICH! (**smooee-neeCH**) Think! SMAOINICH, Thought. SGRIOBH! (**skreev**), Write! SGRIOBH, Wrote.

Times change and so does the way people speak. Long ago they said DO BHRIS, DO CHUIR, etc., where we would now say simply BHRIS, CHUIR, etc., but the DO is put back in again when we are using the little words AN, CHA, GUN and NACH.

Example—AN DO BHRIS E AN COPAN? Did he break the cup? CHA DO BHRIS (E AN COPAN), He did not break the cup. BHA I CINNTEACH NACH DO SGRIOBH I AN LITIR, She was certain that she did not write the letter.

Sometimes, both in speaking and writing the short form D' is used for DO DH'.

Ex. — CHA DO DH' OL E AN CAFE or CHA D' OL E AN CAFE. NACH DO DH' FHAG E AN CAR AIG AN DORUS? or NACH D' FHAG E AN CAR AIG AN DORUS? Did he not leave the car at the door? THAINIG AM POSTA AN DIUGH, The postman came to-day. GUN DO THAINIG AM POSTA AN DIUGH or GUN D' THAINIG AM POSTA AN DIUGH, That the postman came to-day.

Pron. D'OL (**dol**), D' FHAG (**dak**), D' THAINIG (**dan-ik**). POSTA (**posta**), Postman. THAINIG (**han-eek**), came.

Learn these words

BALACH (**ba-laCH**), Boy ; also GILLE.
CATHAIR (**ca-hir**), Chair, also a city.
GU or GUS, to or towards ; also means until.
SEAS! (**shayss**), Stand!
FRANGACH (**frangk-aCH**), Frenchman.
SPAINNTEACH (**spen-chaCH**), Spaniard.

AIR CUAIRT (**er kooirt** or **kooirst**), On a visit.
UBH (**oo**), EGG.
UIBHEAN (**oo-yan**), Eggs.
BRUICH! (**broo-eeCH**), Cook! boil!
SINE (**sheen-a**), Jean.
SRUTH (**sroo**), Stream.
TUIG! (**tooig** nearly **took**), Understand!
POIT (**poch**), Pot.
COIRE (**kora**), kettle.
SUIDH! (**soo-ee**), sit!
A, that (person or thing).
PEANN (**pyaoon**). pen.
IM (**eem**), butter.
CAISE (**kasha**), cheese.
RIOMHACH (**reev-aCH**), luxurious, elegant.
SEACHAD (**sheCH-ad**), past.
RIGH DFORSA (**ree jorsa**), King George.
BAN-RIGH EALASAID (**ban-ree ela-sayj**), Queen
  Elizabeth.
BLATH-AN (**bla-han**), flower-s.
LEABHAR (**lyOr**), book.
TUIT! (**tooch**), fall!
GU or GUS, to.
  Note.— Sound SH and TH like H. RT in some
places is sounded like RST. BH and MH sound as V.
MH in the middle or at the end of a word is like W
usually, but the V sound is quite common. However,
IBH. IMH are generally sounded as "eev". CH always
as in LOCH.

Gaelic to English

  Cuir uisge anns a' choire. Chuir Mairi uisge fuar
anns a' choire. Tog an leabhar. An do thog am
balach an leabhar a bha air a' bhord? Cha do thog.
ach thog e am peann. Shuidh Eilidh anns a' chathair
agus chaidh Morag gus an uinneag. Thuig Anna na
bha am Frangach ag radh ach cha do thuig i an
Spainnteach. Chaidh m' (mo) athair air cuairt do
Eire. An d'fhuair e uibhean? Cha d'fhuair. ach
fhuair e im agus caise. Bhruich i ubh anns a' phoit.

Thuit am balach anns an t-sruth an uair a bha e ag iasgach. Tha Sine ag radh nach d'thainig an duine leis a' ghual an diugh ach gum bheil e coltach gum bi e a' tighinn am maireach. Chaidh car riomhach seachad agus co bha ann ach Righ Deorsa agus Banrigh Ealasaid. Dh'innis e an sgeul sin gu tric. Co spion na blathan boidheach sin? Spion Morag.

Translation

Put water in the kettle. Mary put cold water in the kettle. Lift the book. Did the boy lift the book that was on the table? He did not, but he lifted the pen. Helen sat in the chair and Morag went to the window. Anna understood what the Frenchman was saying but she did not understand the Spaniard. My father went on a visit to Eire. Did he get eggs? He did not, but he got butter and cheese. She boiled an egg in the pot. The boy fell into the stream when he was fishing. Jean says that the man did not come with the coal to-day but that it is likely he'll be coming to-morrow. A luxurious car went past and who was in it but King George and Queen Elizabeth. He told that story often. Who plucked those beautiful flowers? Morag (Sarah).

LESSON 8

We know that when you want to say that a person has anything, you put it as being "at him". Thus THA TAIGH AIG IAIN, A house is at John, or, John has a house. If you replace John by him, this would run, A house is at him, THA TAIGH AIGE, the AIG and E being joined together into one single word. In the same way, I have a house would run, A house is at me, We have a house as, A house is at us, and so on. It is common in all languages for people to cut their words short: for instance in English Will not becomes Won't, and in Scots, With him is shortened to Waem or Wim. Gaelic likewise shortens AIG MI to AGAM, the stress being on the AG of course. Our phrase would be written and spoken thus: THA TAIGH AGAM, I have a house. It might be helpful if we put what we are going to say into a little table.

AIG MI becomes AGAM (**akum**), At me. AIG TU, AGAD (**akut**), At thee. AIG E, AIGE (**eka**), At him or it. AIG I, AICE (**eCH-ka**), At her or it. AIG SINN, AGAINN (**ak-ing**), At us. AIG SIBH, AGAIBH (**ak-iv**), At you. AIG IAD, ACA (**aCH-ka**), At them.

Example — BHA TAIGH MOR ACA AIR AN DUTHAICH, They had a big house in the country.

DUTHAICH (**doo-eeCH**), Country. Notice how Gaelic in this phrase uses **On** where English would say **In.**

Here is a new word for you. It is FIOS (**fiss**), and it means Knowledge, Information, or Word (not A word), Notice. Read the following examples carefully for they are very important.

THA FIOS AGAINN GUM BHEIL AIRGIOD GU LEOIR AGAIBH, We know that you have plenty of money ; or, Knowledge is at us that money galore is at you, AIRGIOD (**erra-gut**), Money. Here is another use. CUIR FIOS AIR AN LIGHICHE. Send for the doctor. (**lyeeCHy**), A Doctor. CO AIG AM BHEIL FIOS, who knows, i.e., at who(m) or Who at is knowledge. CUIR FIOS AIR AN LEABHAR, Send for the book. THUIRT MAIRI GUN DO CHUIR I FIOS AIR AN LEABHAR, Mary said that she sent for the book.

When you wish to say in Gaelic that a person would or would not do something, i.e., Stand, lift, marry, put, break, etc. take the action word and add the letters ADH (**uGH**) to it.

Example — SEAS! (**shayss**), stand! SEASADH (**shayss-uGH**), Would stand. POS! Marry! POSADH (**pos-uGH**), Would marry. TOG! Lift! TOGADH (**tOk-uGH**), Would lift, fair up.

Words where the last vowel is I such as CUIR, BUAIL, SGOILT (**skolch**), add EADH (**uGH**). CUIR, CUIREADH (**kooir-uGH**). So also BUAILEADH, SGOILTEADH (**skolch-uGH**).

Example — THUIRT MAIRI GUN SEASADH I AIG AN DORUS GUS AN TIGEADH AN GILLE LEIS A' BHAINNE, Mary said that she would stand at the door till the boy would come with the milk. TIGEADH (**cheek-uGH**), GUS AN (or AM before B, F, M, P), until. GUS (**gooss**).

Note. — BITHEADH (**be-uGH**) is often written BIODH (also **be-uGH**). FIOS also as FHIOS (**iss**) i.e., CHAN 'EIL FHIOS AGAM, I don't know.

Learn these words

PIOB (**peep**), Pipe. TOMBACA (**tom-baCH-ka**), Tobacco. CUIR FIOS DO (or GU), Send word to. THA DOCHAS AGAM, I have hope ; or THA MI AN DOCHAS, I am in hope ; both mean I hope. DOCHAS (**doCHas**), Hope. TIG (**cheek**), Will come. TIGEADH, Would come. FHUAIR FIOS, Got word.

RUIG (**rooeeg**), Will reach, arrive. RUIGEADH, Would reach, arrive. CIOBAIR (**keeper**), Shepherd. TOGADH, Would lift. THU (also TU) meaning thou or thee is used familiarly: but SIBH to elders or strangers.

ROIMH FHADA (**roee ada**), before long.
AIG AN TAIGH, at home.
O'N TAIGH, from home.
CUIDEACHD (**kooj-eCHk**), also.
GREUSAICHE (**gray-seeCHy**), shoemaker.
BROG-AN, shoe-s.
MU OCHD UAIREAN (**moo oCHk ooran**), about eight o'clock.
GU CINNTEACH, certainly.
GUN TIG (**cheek**), that (he) will come.
AIR BALL (**ba-ool**), immediately.
AN TIOTAN (**tyoo-tan**), in a jiffy.
GRADH (**gra**, DH silent, also **graGH**), love.
NIGHEAN, girl, daughter.
AITIDH (**ach-ee**), damp.
GLASCHU (**glasa-CHu**), Glasgow.

Gaelic to English

Tha piob aig Iain ach chan 'eil tombaca aige. Am bheil cu agaibh aig an taigh? Tha, agus cat cuideachd. An robh fios aca gun robh sinn a' tighinn? Cha robh. Bha iad o'n taigh. Chuir an greusaiche fios gu Anna nach biodh na brogan deas roimh a' mhaduinn. Tha an duine bochd seo tinn. An cuir sibh fios air an lighiche? Cuiridh, gu cinnteach. Tha dochas agam gun tig e air ball. Thuirt Sine gum posadh i Domhnall ciobar aig Nollaig. Tha e ag radh gun ol e am bainne. Bha e ag radh gun oladh e am bainne. Bha e ag radh (also Thuirt e) gun d'ol e am bainne. Bidh mi agad an tiotan. Bha gradh aige do'n nighean sin. Thuirt e nach fanadh e fada anns an taigh aitidh sin. Bha e fliuch anns a' mhaduinn ach bha an ciobair cinnteach gun togadh e roimh fhada. Bha an dochas gun ruigeadh e Glaschu mu ochd uairean.

Translation to English

John has a pipe but he has no(t) tobacco. Have you a dog at home? There is (yes) and a cat also. Did they know that we were coming? They did not (no). They were from home. The shoemaker sent word to Anna that the shoes would not be ready before the morning. This poor man is ill. Will you send for the doctor? I will, certainly. I hope that he will come immediately. Jean said that she would marry Donald (the) shepherd at Christmas. He says that he will drink the milk. He was saying that he would drink the milk. He was saying that he drank the milk. I'll be with (at) you in a jiffy. He was in love with (he had love to) that girl. He said that he wouldn't remain long in that damp house. It was wet in the morning but the shepherd was certain that it would fair up before lang. He was hoping that he would reach Glasgow about eight o'clock.

LESSON 9

We were speaking in the last lesson about "should" and "would" when preceded by That or That Not. For example, THUIRT E GUM POSADH E MAIRI, He said that he would marry Mary. Let us put this in question form: AM POSADH E MAIRI? Would he marry Mary? or NACH POSADH E MAIRI? Would he not marry Mary? Suppose he won't, we say CHA PHOSADH, He would not. Remember that CHA wherever possible sharpens (puts an H after) the first letter of the following word. If, however, he would, we say PHOSADH (E MAIRI). PHOSADH you will notice is the same as the past time of POS with ADH added. Thus PHOS E, He married: PHOSADH E, He would marry. In the same way we have THOGADH E, He would lift: CHUIREADH E, He would put and so on. By the way, notice the E in EADH coming after the I in CHUIR.

Remember, however, that after AN(AM), NACH, GUN(GUM), MUR (unless), NAN (if), we use the UNsharpened forms only, i.e., POSADH, TOGADH, CUIREADH, etc.

If your word begins with a vowel or F followed by a vowel do what you did with action words in past time. DH'OL AN CAT AM BAINNE, The cat drank the milk. DH'OLADH AN CAT AM BAINNE, The cat would drink the milk. DH'ITH E, He ate. DH'ITHEADH AN DUINE NA BHA AIR A' BHORD, The man would eat what was on the table. DH'ITHEADH (yeeCH-uGH).

But GUN, etc., OLADH, ITHEADH.

When I or We come into our phrase we often use a special form. For example, instead of POSADH MI we may say POSAINN and PHOSADH MI would be PHOSAINN (fos-ing). POSADH SINN would be

34

POSAMAID (**pos-a-mij**) and PHOSADH SINN, PHOSAMAID (**fos-a-mij**). For words like CUIR, BRIS, etc., we add INN and EAMAID.

Example — B(H)RISINN (**breesh-ing, vreesh-ing**), B(H)RISEAMAID (**breesh-a-mij, vreesh-a-mij**). I would break, we would break.

DH'OLAINN, DH'OLAMAID, I, We, would drink. (**GHol-ing. GHol-a-mij**).

GUN OLAINN, OLAMAID. That I, we would drink.

Words like LEUM! (**lyaym**), Leap! Ruith! (**roo-eeCH**), Run! SGOILT! (**skolch**), Split! should give you no trouble. LEUMAINN, I would leap and GUN LEUMAINN, That I would leap. These words begin with L; N, R ; also S followed by G, M, P, T (**GuMPoT**).

Here is an interesting type of phrase.

CHAN 'EIL FIOS AGAM AM BI E A' TIGHINN or CHAN 'EIL FIOS AGAM AN TIG E.

I don't know whether he will be coming (or whether he will come). But if we turn it direct from Gaelic to English it would run, I don't know Will he be coming i.e., the answer to a question. Again CHAN 'EIL MI CINNTEACH AN ROBH E AIR A' BHANAIS. I am not sure Was he at the wedding: or in more correct English, I am nòt sure whether he was at the wedding. BANAIS (**ban-ish**), wedding. Note AIR on, and not AIG is used here. If we want to use "Whether or not" we employ CO DHIUBH (**ko-yoo**) which means "Which of them": and this is how we put our phrase. CHAN 'EIL MI CINNTEACH CO DHIUBH BHA E AIR A' BHANAIS NO NACH ROBH. I am not sure whether (which of them) he was at the wedding or that he was not.

AM BHEIL FIOS AGAIBH CO DHIUBH BIDH AR CAIRDEAN A' TIGHINN NO NACH BI. Do you know whether (which of them) our friends will be coming or that they will not be, i.e., whether or not they will be coming. CAIRDEAN (**kar-jayn**), friends.

35

Learn these words

MORAN, Many.
INBHIR AIR, Ayr.
TRATH (**tra**), early.
BHITHINN (**vee-ing**), I should or would be.
BHITHEAMAID (**vee-a-mij**), We should or would be.
IARR AIR (**eer er**), ask, request, followed by "on".
BEAN AN TAIGHE (**ben an ta-ee**), the housewife.
DORUS-CUIL (**kool**), back door.
NAN (or NAM), if.
MUR (sometimes followed by AN or AM) unless, if not.
SUIL (**sool**), eye.
DEISE (**jay-sha**), suit of clothes.
ITH (**eeCH**), eat.
DEAN CABHAG (**jayn cafag**), make haste.
DEAN, also means "do"
EOGHANN (**yO-an**), Ewen.
GU TOILEACH (**goo tolaCH**), willingly.
DAONNAN (**doon-an**), always.
RO (**ro**), too, rather.
LAIDIR (**la-jir**), strong.
COSNADH (**kos-nuGH**), job, employment.
COMA (**kOma**), indifferent.
GABH AIR, punish, i.e., go for (on).   GABH also
  means take.
SGOILEAR (**skolar**), scholar.

Gaelic to English

Cha chuirinn moran earbsa anns an duine sin.
Thuirt e gun ruigeamaid Inbhir-air trath 'san (anns an)
la.   Bhithinn toilichte nan gabhadh sibh an leabhar.
Dh' iarr bean an taighe air an duine a bhi cinnteach
gum fagadh ean gual aig an dorus-cuil.   Bhualadh
Seumas an cu mur cumainn suil air.   C'ar son nach
'eil Niall a tighinn do'n eaglais?   Tha e ag radh gun
tigeadh e nan robh deise ur aige.   Dh'olamaid copan
te gu toileach ach chan olamaid an cafe a dheanadh
Eoghann a chionn gum bheil e daonnan ro laidir.   Co

dhiubh fhuair e cosnadh no nach d'fhuair tha mi
coma. Thuirt am maighstir gun gabhadh e air na
sgoilearan mur deanadh iad cabhag. Chuirinn geall
air an each sin nan robh mi cinnteach gun ruitheadh e.

Translation

I wouldn't put much trust in that man. He said
that we would reach Ayr early in the day. I should
be pleased if you would take the book. The housewife
asked the man to be sure to leave the coal at the
back-door. James would hit the dog unless I kept
(would keep) an eye on him. Why is Neil not coming
to the church? He says that he would come if he
had a new suit. We would drink a cup of tea willingly
(with pleasure) but we would not drink the coffee
that Ewen would make because it is always too
strong. Whether he got a job (employment) or not
I don't care (am indifferent). The master said that
he would punish the scholars if they would not hurry
up. I would put a bet on that horse if I were sure
that it would run.

LESSON 10

In lesson 8 we saw how AIG, At could be joined up with MI, TU, etc., to form one word AGAM, AGAD and so on. The same thing happens with other little words and of these one of the commonest is AIR, On. It changes more than AIG but isn't really difficult. Here it is:—AIR MI becomes **ORM** (as in **Form**), On me. AIR TU, **ORT** (as in **Fort**), On thee. AIR E, **AIR** (**er** as in **Term**), On him (it). AIR I, **OIRRE** (**urra**), On her (it). AIR SINN, **OIRNN** (**or-ing**), On us. AIR SIBH, **OIRBH** (**or-iv**), On you. AIR IAD, **ORRA** (as in **Corral**), On them.

In some places ORT is sounded like **Orst,** an S sound being put in between R and T. This happens with many other words. Note also that AIR means both **ON** and **On him** or **On it.**

Learn these words

ACRAS (**aCH-kras**), Hunger ; TART, Thirst ; also PATHADH (**pa-uGH**), Thirst ; FUACHD (**foo-aCHk**), Cold ; EAGAL (**ek-al**), Fear ; CADAL (**ka-dal**), Sleep. This is how they are used and others like them.

THA CADAL ORM, I am sleepy, Sleep is on me ; BHA FUACHD TROM AIR, He had a heavy cold, i.e., A heavy cold was on him ; BHA EAGAL OIRNN NACH TIGEADH E, We were afraid that he would not come ; THUIRT NA GILLEAN GUN ROBH PATHADH (TART) ORRA, The boys said that they were thirsty ; AM BHEIL ACRAS (or AN T-ACRAS) OIRBH? Are you hungry?

You may often hear folk saying AM BHEIL AN CADAL ORT? or AM PATHADH, AN TART, etc., Is **the** sleep, **the** thirst, etc., on you, much as you would say in English, Have you **a** cold or **the** cold?

Some other useful phrases are:—THA MEAS MOR AGAM AIR, I have a great respect for him, i.e., A great respect is at me on him ; MEAS (**mayss**), Respect, Esteem. AM BHEIL FEUM AGAIBH AIR?

Do you need it? FEUM (**faym**), Need, Use ; THA AITHNE AGAM ORRA, I am acquainted with them ; AITHNE (**en-ya**), Acquaintance with a person, place or thing ; FIOS means knowledge of a fact so don't be mixing it up with AITHNE.

Instead of using AITHNE we might have put it in this way: THA MI EOLACH ORRA where EOLACH (**yo-laCH**) means Acquainted or informed. DUINE EOLACH means A well-informed man.

Here is a topical one: THA TAIGH A DHITH ORM, I want or require a house ; A DHITH (**a ye**), Required or Wanting. DE THA A' CUR DRAGH OIRRE? What is worrying her? DRAGH (**druGH**), Annoyance or Worry ; DE? (**jay**), What?

Note—CUIR ! Put, but CUR, putting.

Now study the following ones carefully.

THA AIRGIOD AGAM AIR, I have money on him, that is, He owes me money ; NACH ROBH COIG PUNND AGAIBH AIR MAIRI? Wasn't there £5 at you on Mary? Didn't Mary owe you £5?

Have you ever heard a Scots phrase like " Oh the little rascal drank all the milk on me " ? The **on me** of course means **to my loss.** This comes out of the Gaelic and is used very commonly.

DH' OL AN CAT AM BAINNE ORM, The cat drank the milk (on me), i.e., to my loss. DH' FHALBH AM BATA ORRA, The boat went off on them, they missed the boat.

And this one now: AN GABH SIBH FICHEAD PUNND AIR AN EACH SIN? Will you take £20 for (on) that horse? FICHEAD (**feeCH-ud**), Twenty.

Learn these words

FIODH (**fyuGH**), Wood, timber ; ORD (**ord**), Hammer ; TARRANG (**tar-rung**), Nail ; TAIRNEAN (**tara-nyan**), Nails ; GABH SRAID (**gav sraj**), Take a walk ; SRAID (**sraj**) also means street ; O CHIONN (**CHyun**) FADA for a long time ; CO? Who? TRI (**tree**), Three ; GU MATH, Fairly or Well ; TRANG,

busy; MISE (**meesh a**), stronger form than MI;
CEUD (**kayud**), Hundred; TUILLIDH AGUS SIN,
More than that, TUILLIDH (**tool-ye**), more; COIG
PUNND (**kO-ik poont**); OCHD (**oCHk**), eight;
IARRAIDH (**ee-ary**) asking, requesting.

Gaelic to English

Am bheil pathadh ort, Iain? Chan 'eil ach tha acras
(or **an t-acras**) orm. Tha mi duilich gun bheil fuachd
trom oirre. De tha a dhith air na gillean a nis? Tha
iad ag iarraidh dol (**to go**) a mach anns a' bhata. Thuirt
an saor gun robh feum aige air fiodh, ord agus tairnean.
Mur 'eil cabhag ort, Alasdair, gabhaidh sinn sraid anns
a' phairc. Mur dean sinn cabhag, falbhaidh am bata
oirnn. "Co dh'ith an siucar orm?" thuirt Mairi. "Dh'ith
mise," fhreagair Domhnall, "agus tha mi duilich gun do
chuir mi dragh oirbh." Dh'iarr an duine uasal air
Seumas a radh, an gabhadh e ceud punnd air a' char;
ach bha Seumas ag iarraidh tuillidh agus sin air.

Tha aithne againn air an duine sin o chionn fada
ach chan 'eil meas againn air idir. Tha ochd punnd
againn air. Am bheil sibh eolach air Iain Ruadh? Tha,
gu math eolach, agus air a athair cuideachd. Na bi cur
dragh orm, Eilidh. Tha mi gu math trang an drasda.

Translation

Are you thirsty John? I am not but I am hungry.
I am sorry that she has a heavy cold on her. What are
the boys wanting now? They are asking to go out in
the boat. The joiner said that he needed wood, a
hammer and nails. If you are not in a hurry, Alexander,
we'll take a walk in the park. If we don't hurry up the
boat will go away on us, i.e., we will lose the boat.
"Who ate the (my) sugar?" said Mary. "I did,"
answered Donald, "and I am sorry that I annoyed you."
The gentleman asked James to say if he would take a
hundred pounds for the car; but James was wanting
more than that for it. We know that man for a long
time but we have no respect for him at all. He owes
us eight pounds. Do you know Red John? Yes, fairly
well and his father besides. Don't bother me Helen.
I am fairy busy just now.